SHOW ME GEOGRAPHY

OCEANS

By
Emilie Dufresne

BookLife
PUBLISHING

©2019
BookLife Publishing Ltd.
King's Lynn
Norfolk PE30 4LS
All rights reserved.
Printed in Malaysia.

A catalogue record for this
book is available from the
British Library.

ISBN: 978-1-78637-801-9

Written by:
Emilie Dufresne

Edited by:
Madeline Tyler

Designed by:
Gareth Liddington

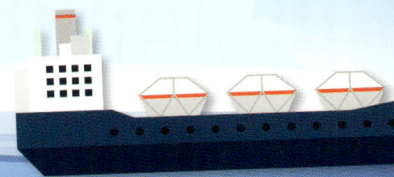

Contents

Words that look like this can be found in the glossary on page 24.

What Is an Ocean?

An ocean is a very large body of salt water. The world has five oceans. These are:

Arctic Ocean

Atlantic Ocean

Pacific Ocean

Indian Ocean

Southern Ocean

Seas are smaller than oceans and are sometimes surrounded by land.

The Mediterranean Sea is a sea surrounded by Europe, Africa and the Middle East. It is almost completely surrounded by land.

Mediterranean Sea

The Water Cycle

The water on Earth is constantly moving and it is always being <u>recycled</u>. This is called the water cycle.

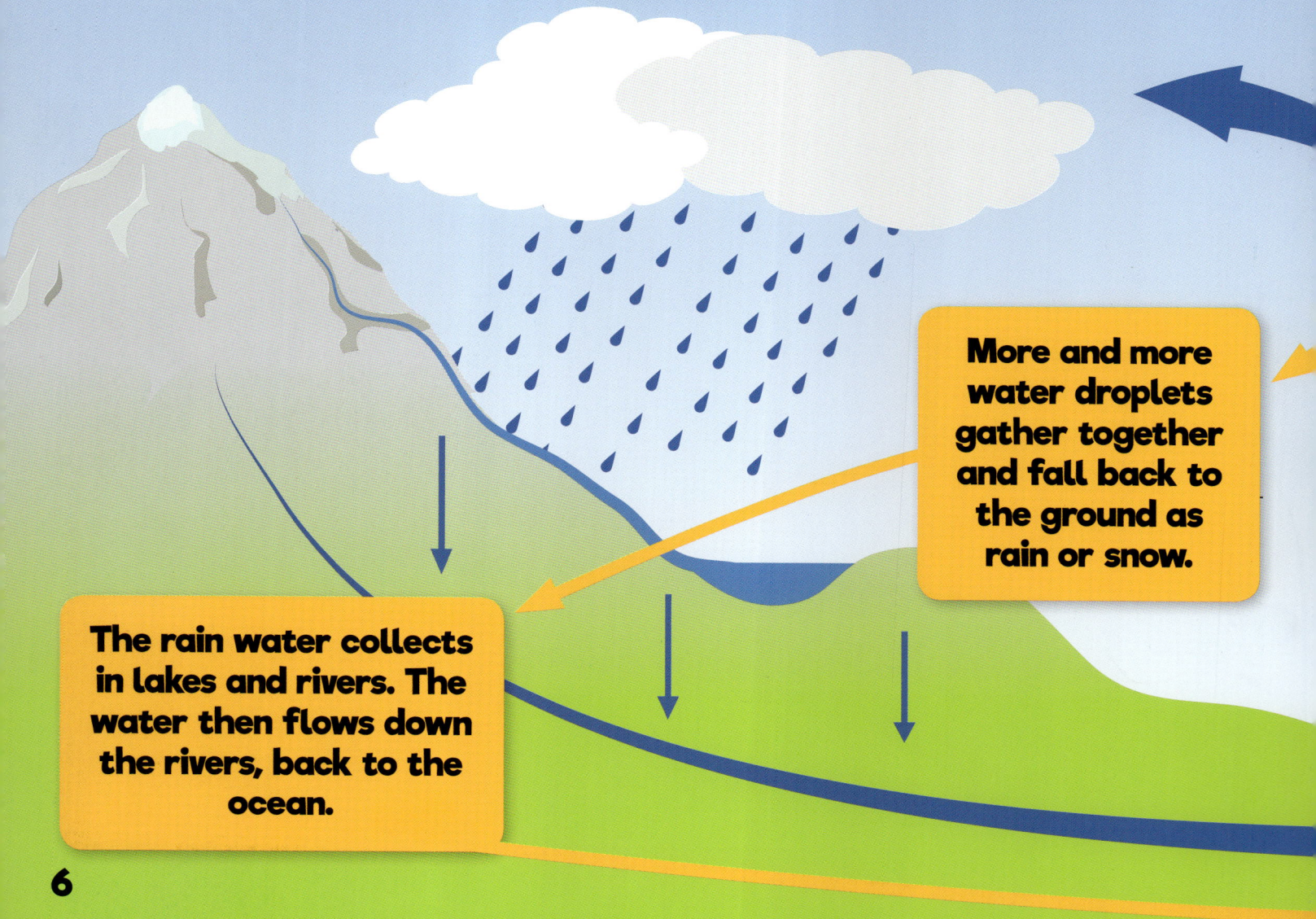

More and more water droplets gather together and fall back to the ground as rain or snow.

The rain water collects in lakes and rivers. The water then flows down the rivers, back to the ocean.

The water _vapour_ in the air cools down and changes into tiny water droplets, making clouds.

The Sun heats up the water in the oceans. This _evaporates_ the water and turns it into vapour in the air.

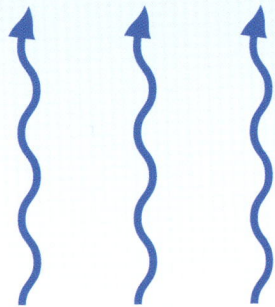

Icebergs

Icebergs are large pieces of ice that separate from ice sheets or glaciers. They float in the water. Usually only a small part of the iceberg can be seen above the water.

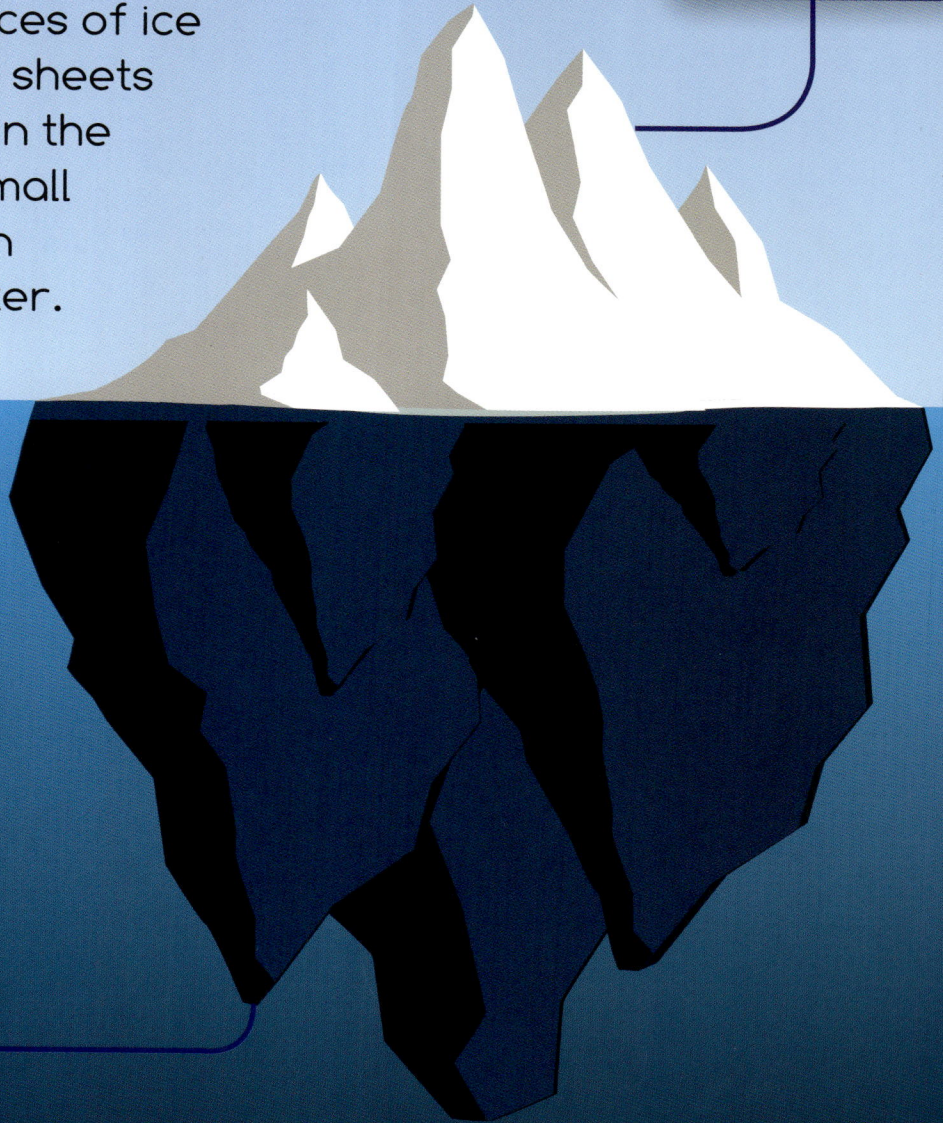

Above water

The larger part of an iceberg is underwater.

Below water

Icebergs can be very big or very small. One of the largest icebergs in the world separated from an ice sheet in Antarctica. It was around the same size as the US state of Connecticut.

Connecticut

The iceberg compared to Connecticut

Set Sail

Mapping and measuring the ocean is very different to mapping and measuring land. This is because there are not as many landmarks at sea.

I think we are lost...

Sailors can find out where they are by using lines of latitude and longitude. These are invisible lines that run around the Earth, from north to south and from east to west.

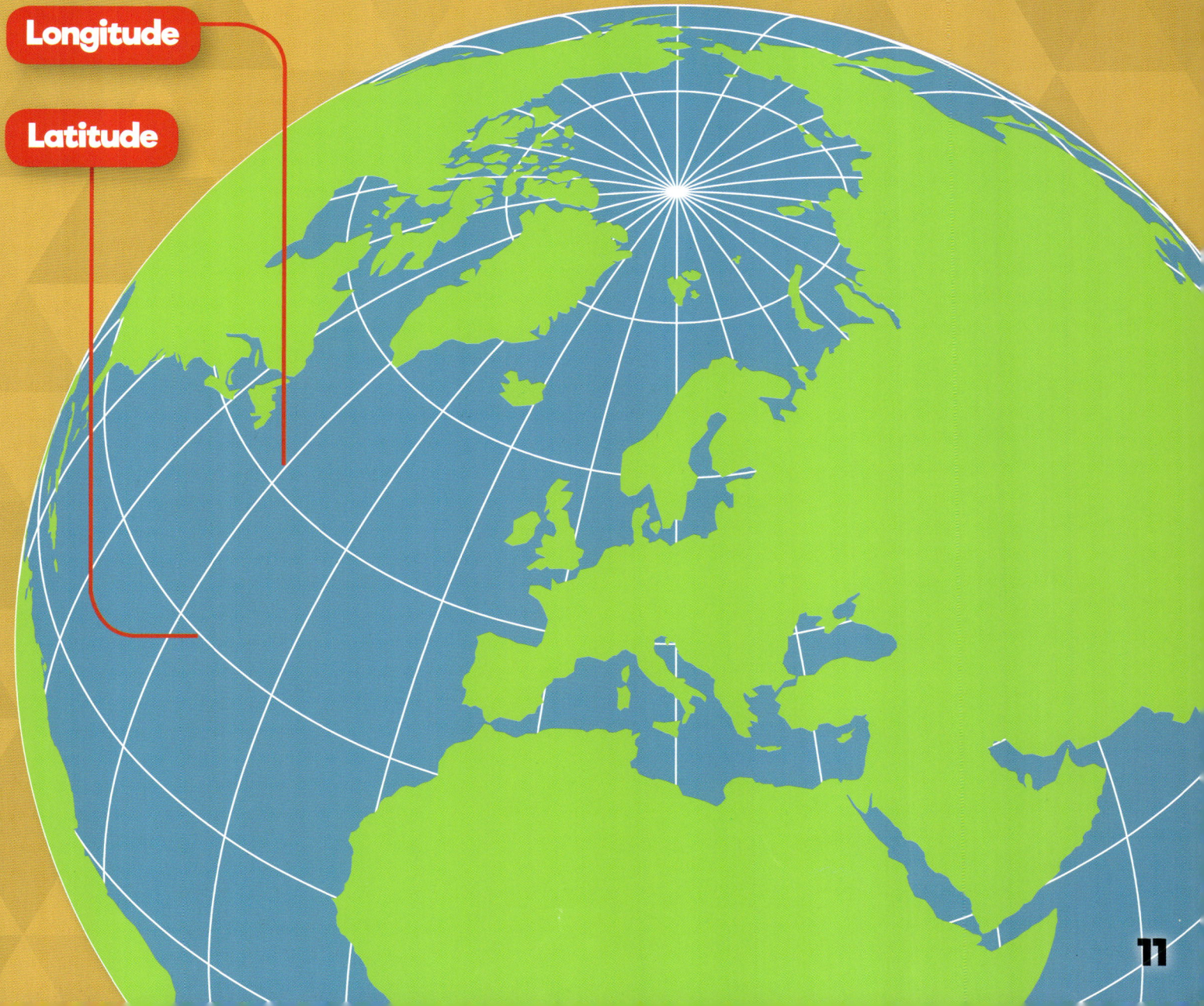

Longitude

Latitude

Ocean Explorers

Sylvia Earle is an explorer who studies the ocean and works to protect it.

She holds the record for the deepest solo dive. She dived down over 380 metres.

In 2012, James Cameron took a <u>submersible</u> called Deepsea Challenger to the bottom of the Mariana Trench in the Pacific Ocean. This is the deepest part of the ocean and it is called Challenger Deep.

Ocean Depths

The ocean has five zones at different depths. Each zone is home to different animals and plants.

Dolphins

Sunlight Zone – This zone gets the most sunlight. Most ocean life lives here.

0–200 METRES

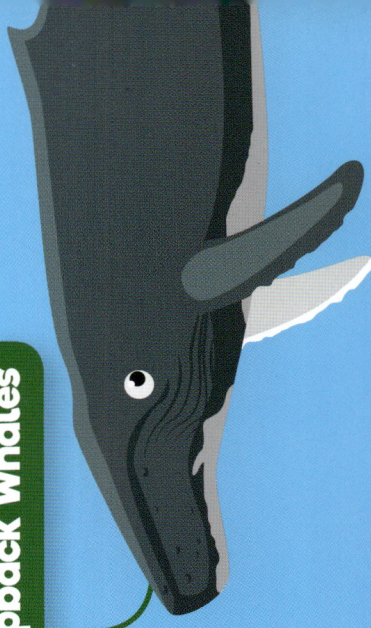

Humpback whales

Octopuses

Twilight Zone – Less sunlight reaches here. The water is much colder.

200–1,000 METRES

Midnight Zone – No sunlight reaches this zone.

Giant squid

Anglerfish

Giant tube worms

Sea spiders

Abyss – Temperatures here are near to freezing.

Snailfish

Sea cucumbers

Trenches – Scientists need special equipment to explore the very cold and very dark trenches in the ocean floor.

Life in the Ocean

GOBLIN SHARK
When hunting, these sharks' jaws can slide forwards away from their bodies to catch <u>prey</u>.

LEAFY SEA DRAGON
These animals are well <u>camouflaged</u> by the seaweed that they live in, which hides them from <u>predators</u>.

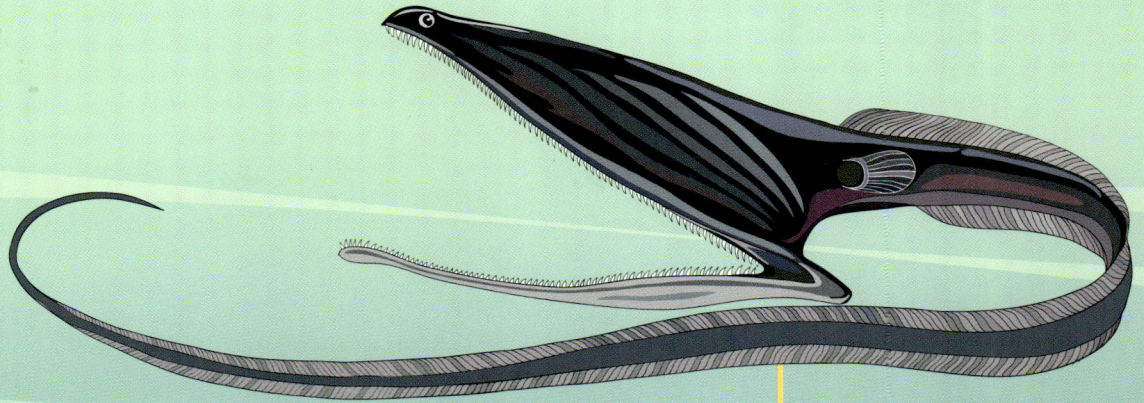

GULPER EEL
Gulper eels have jaws that can gulp down large prey, making their heads swell up a bit like a balloon.

GIANT ISOPOD
These <u>crustaceans</u> live on the ocean floor and are around 30 centimetres long.

Only five percent of the ocean floor has been explored. Who knows what else might be lurking down there?

Coral Reefs

Coral reefs can be found in the ocean. They are made of lots of living creatures that are hard, like skeletons.

Coral reefs are home to many different plants and creatures, which makes them very important to the ocean.

Coral reefs are also home to over one-quarter of all ocean life even though they cover less than two percent of the ocean floor.

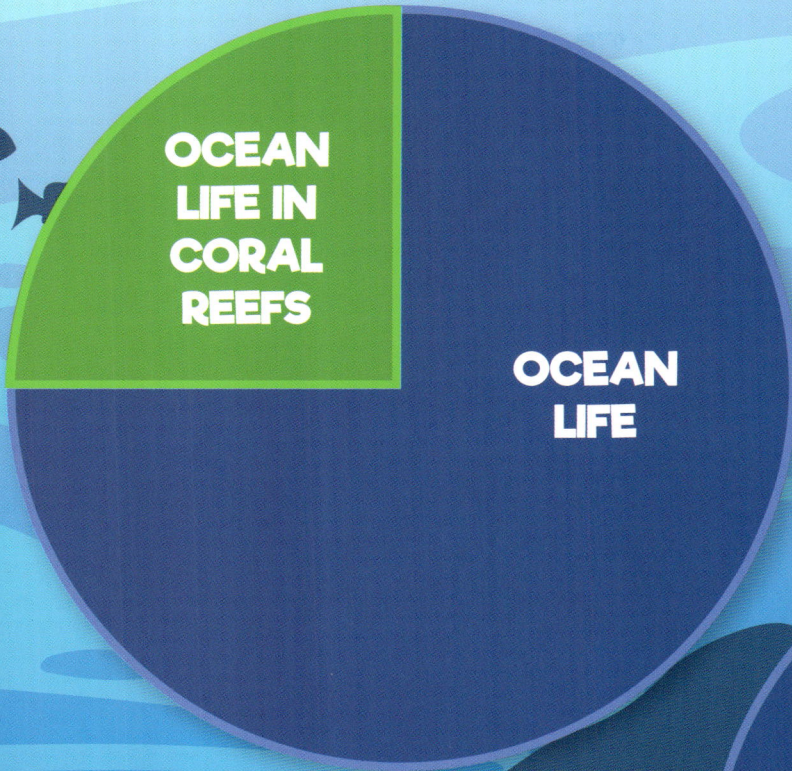

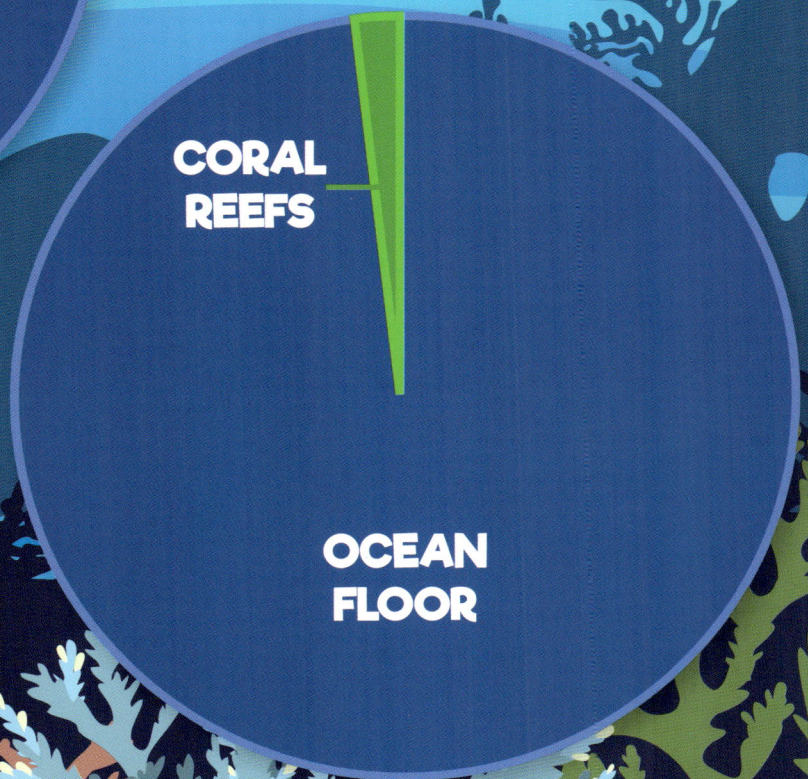

OCEAN LIFE IN CORAL REEFS

OCEAN LIFE

CORAL REEFS

OCEAN FLOOR

Oceans under Threat

Lots of things that humans do are bad for the ocean.

Overfishing can take away food from other sea animals and make it hard for certain animals to survive.

Lots of **plastic** ends up in our oceans. Animals can eat the plastic, thinking it is food. This can kill them.

Global warming is the warming of the Earth, mostly because of human actions. Warmer water can make it hard for certain animals to live in or near the oceans and can even kill coral reefs.

Guess the Depth

Can you match the animal
with the right depth?

1. Octopus

2. Anglerfish

3. Sea cucumber

4. Dolphin

A. Sunlight

B. Twilight

C. Midnight

D. Trenches

Glossary

camouflaged	hidden by blending in with its surroundings
crustaceans	animals that live in water and have a hard outer shell
equipment	items that are needed to complete a certain job
evaporates	turns from a liquid into a gas or vapour, usually through heat
landmarks	objects that help people know where they are
predators	animals that eat other animals for food
prey	animals that are eaten by other animals for food
recycled	used again to make something else
submersible	a ship built to travel and work deep underwater
vapour	tiny parts of a solid or liquid that float in the air as a gas, such as mist or steam

Index

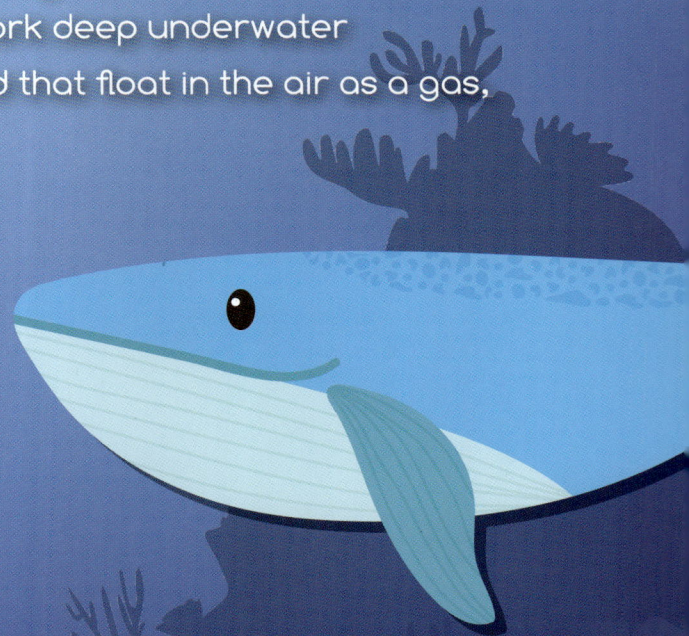

How do
PLANTS GROW?

First published in 2018 by Wayland
Copyright © Hodder and Stoughton 2018

Managing editor: Victoria Brooker
Creative design: Paul Cherrill

ISBN: 978 1 5263 0664 7

Printed in China

FSC
www.fsc.org
MIX
Paper from
responsible sources
FSC® C104740

Wayland is a division of
Hachette Children's Books,
an Hachette UK company.
www.hachette.co.uk

How do
PLANTS GROW?

Written by
KAY BARNHAM

Illustrated by
MIKE GORDON

WAYLAND

'We're going to do something really amazing,'
Mrs Wakefield said to the class one morning.
'Are we going on a school trip
to the moon?' asked Adam.

The teacher laughed. 'Not today,' she said.
'But we are going to plant our very own seeds.'
'What's amazing about that?' said Adam.
'Just wait and see,' said Mrs Wakefield.

'Seeds come in all shapes and sizes,'
said the teacher. She showed them a pea,
an avocado stone, an apple pip, a coffee bean,
a pine cone, a chickpea and a walnut.

'Are you sure these are all seeds?' asked Adam. 'They look so different.'

Mrs Wakefield nodded. 'Different types of seeds grow into different plants,' she said.

'Look,' said Mrs Wakefield, opening one hand. Striped seeds lay on her palm. 'We're going to grow these seeds.'
'What are they?' asked Adam's friend, Zayn.

'It's a surprise,' said the teacher.
'I hope they're Jack-and-the-beanstalk seeds,'
Zayn whispered.
Adam giggled.

The teacher gave each of the children
a plant pot. They filled them with soil and
Mrs Wakefield dropped a seed in each one.

Adam sprinkled more soil into his plant pot, so that the seed was hidden. Then he watered it. 'Now, we wait for the seeds to grow,' said Mrs Wakefield.

'How does the seed grow?' asked Adam,
peering into his plant pot.
'Inside the seed coat, there is a baby plant,'
said Mrs Wakefield. 'There's food too.'

'When the seed is warm and wet, the plant uses the food to grow. First, roots appear. Then a stem grows. Leaves grow too.'

'I wish the plant would hurry up,'
said Adam.

'It's going to take a few days before the shoot appears,' said Mrs Wakefield. 'So while the seed is growing, let's think of different sorts of plants.'

'Is a tree a plant?' asked Zayn.
'Yes!' said the teacher. 'Let's go outside and look at some.'

'Some trees are deciduous,' said Mrs Wakefield. 'They lose their leaves every autumn and grow new leaves in the spring. Can you name some deciduous trees?'

'Oak trees!' said Adam. 'They have huge trunks.'
'Apple trees!' said Zayn. 'That's where apples grow!'
'Look,' said Adam, 'their leaves are
different shapes.'

'Some trees are evergreen,' said the teacher. 'Can you guess what that means?' 'Are they always green...?' asked Adam.

'Yes!' said the teacher. 'Evergreen trees have green leaves all through the year. Fir trees are evergreens. Trees that grow in rainforests are evergreens too.'

The children learnt that some
plants grow in the wild.
'Daisies, dandelions and buttercups are
wildflowers,' said the teacher. 'They grow
where the conditions are right for them.'

'Who looks after them?' asked Adam.
'No one,' said the teacher.
'They don't need any care at all.'

The teacher explained that plants
in gardens often come from somewhere else.
'Garden plants need to be looked after,' she said.

'For example, if they come from a hot country and they are planted in a cold country, then they need to be kept warm in a greenhouse.'

After school, Adam and his mum went to their allotment. Plants grew in neat rows.
'What are these?' asked Adam.

'I'm growing onions, carrots and potatoes for dinner,' Mum said, pointing to them. And I'm growing strawberries for dessert!'

'This is better than a supermarket,' said Adam.
'It's a lot cheaper!' Mum laughed.

25

At school, a green shoot appeared in Adam's plant pot. 'Hurray!' he said. 'At last!' The children's plants grew taller and taller and taller. Soon, they were taller than the children. Leaves grew.

At the top of each plant, petals
opened and a flower appeared.
'Now do you know what these plants are?'
asked Mrs Wakefield.
'Sunflowers!' chorused the pupils.

'This flower is nearly as big as my head!'
said Adam, and everyone laughed.
Mrs Wakefield pointed to the middle
of Adam's flower.

'Look, there are hundreds of
sunflower seeds,' she said. 'If we plant
them, new sunflowers will grow!'
'Wow,' said Adam. 'Plants really are amazing.'

NOTES FOR PARENTS AND TEACHERS

The aim of this book is to introduce children to scientific concepts in an entertaining, informative way. Here are some ideas for activities that will encourage them to think further about plants — and have fun doing it!

ACTIVITIES

1. Go on a nature walk with your class. Count how many different plants you can find. Look out for deciduous and evergreen trees!

2. Cut out plant pictures from magazines and make a plant collage. Include flowers, trees, shrubs and plants from all over the world.

3 Can you rearrange these anagrams to find five phrases to do with plants?

ICED DUO US

SWIRLED WOLF

OATS POET

NEWS FLOUR

TALON MELT

DECIDUOUS, WILDFLOWERS, POTATOES, SUNFLOWER, ALLOTMENT

GROW YOUR OWN SUNFLOWER!

Put a few pebbles at the bottom of a plant pot. Fill the pot nearly to the top with soil. Then drop a sunflower seed on top and add a little more soil.

Put the plant pot in a sunny place. Remember to water your sunflower every day. After a few days, a shoot will appear!

As your sunflower grows taller, tie the stem to a stick or a cane. This will stop it falling over.

DID YOU KNOW ...?

The tallest tree in the world is a giant redwood, somewhere in California, USA. It is nearly 116 metres tall. To keep it safe, only a few people know exactly where it is ...

Some plants eat meat! A Venus flytrap is a plant that eats flies and other small insects.

There are about 400,000 different types of plant in the world.

BOOKS TO SHARE

Plants
(*Boom Science* series)
by Georgia Amson-Bradshaw
(Wayland, 2018)

The Amazing Life Cycle of Plants
(*Look and Wonder* series)
by Kay Barnham
(Wayland, 2018)

Seed Safari
(*Plant Life* series)
by Judith Heneghan
(Wayland, 2018)

Plants
(*The Curiosity Box* series)
by Peter Riley
(Watts Publishing, 2016)